Table of Contents

What types of cannabis businesses can I start?

You have many paths to pursue in the cannabis industry. Here are three main categories to start with.

Grow it

You can start a marijuana cultivation business, meaning you're growing cannabis for the masses to consume. To do this, you'll need knowledge of cannabis horticulture. If you don't have that expertise, hire someone who does.

For a wholesale cannabis operation, you'll pay an average of $42 per square foot in startup expenses. This money goes toward lights, air circulation, electricity, seeds and other costs. The median startup costs and annual operating expenses for a wholesale cultivation business is $400,000.

How do I start a weed farm?

What you need to start a farm varies depending on where you live and what type of farm you want to start.

Generally, you'll need to buy real estate for your grow space and put together a business plan before applying for permits required by your state. In California, this means applying for a cannabis cultivation license with the Department of Food and Agriculture there are several different types of licenses, depending on where you plan on growing your bud. Then, you'll need to get together the funds to buy equipment needed to grow cannabis in your space, which widely varies depending on how you grow your product. This can include security, seeds, lighting and more. Once you're all set up, you can start growing your plants.

Create infused products

Infused products are products combined with marijuana oils, such as edibles, botanicals, lotions, ointments, beverages and tinctures. This could be a big market. In 2016, businesses selling cannabis-infused food, beverages and cosmetics cashed in to the tune of $180 million and that's just in California. With a median startup cost and annual operating expenses of $250,000, infused-product manufacturing businesses are typically less expensive than cultivation operations, requiring a median $250,000 to start up and operate annually.

Start a store

In the cannabis industry, retail locations are known as collectives or dispensaries. They're places where consumers can get cannabis safely and legally most notably for medical reasons.

You may need to jump through regulatory hoops to start a dispensary, such as submitting an application and paying a licensing fee. However, a retail business can pay off big, especially as more consumers look for legitimate places to obtain cannabis. The median startup costs and annual operating expenses for medical dispensaries and recreational stores is around $193,000.

Steps to start a cannabis business

Ready to start your cannabis business? Follow these steps to get up and running.

1. Conduct preliminary research.

Before going all in with your business, see whether it's a venture you really want to pursue.

The legal arena is a good place to start your research:

- Familiarize yourself with federal cannabis laws.
- Research your state's laws for marijuana consumption and starting a business.
- Find out which licenses and permits you need.

Learn about your financing options and consider how your business will manage its finances. It's all but impossible to get a loan from an FDIC-insured bank, as financial institutions are rightfully wary of violating federal law. Many banks even refuse deposits from cannabis businesses. That's a big reason an estimated 70% of cannabis businesses don't have bank accounts.

It's restrictions like these that make it difficult to start a cannabis business. Before pouring resources into your venture, understand what you're getting into. You could save a lot of time and energy you'd otherwise lose by diving in headfirst.

2. **Create a business plan.**

Writing a business plan will help you gauge the feasibility of your venture. Its contents might include:

- A company description. Clarify what your business does and who it serves. Consider which competitive advantages your business will have.
- Market analysis. Is there a great market need for your business? Who will be your competitors? Are there trends that your business is looking to capitalize on?
- Organization and management.Choose a legal structure for your business. Create an organizational chart to show who will lead your business.

- Marketing and sales. How will you find customers, and what defines a sale or the point at which you make money in your business?
- Financial projections. What will your revenue and expenses look like? Make financial forecasts for at least the next three years, and explain why they make sense.

If you're writing a business plan to seek funding, include a funding request section. Here, you'll describe how much funding you'll need, what you need it for and how you'll deploy the capital.

3.Choose a location.

Location is especially important if you're opening a dispensary, as you want a place that's easily accessible by your target market.

Even if foot traffic isn't your primary concern, pay attention to your city and county's zoning laws. They can greatly affect where you can locate your business.

Rent may be a factor as well, as it'll eat into your revenue. Picking the right location may help you keep expenses low.

4. **Get the legal basics squared away.**

After you've decided on the legal structure for your business, file the appropriate paperwork with your state's government and pay any required fees. Apply for permits and licenses relevant to your state.

After you've received permission from your state government to pursue a cannabis operation, check that your business will comply with your state's regulations.

With so much at stake, it may be worth getting advice from a lawyer.

5. **Build your business.**

After completing the four previous steps, you'll have created a legal business. Now, it's time to start making money.

Decide where to focus your efforts to build out your business. This could include:

- Developing your operating space. Activate utilities, sign a lease for retail space or a warehouse, buy merchandising equipment and invest in technology.
- Forming partnerships.Your business will need the help of vendors,

contractors and other partners. If you run a retail shop, you may want to pursue relationships with product wholesalers and cultivators.

- Marketing. Get the word out about your business. A few avenues you can start with include online advertising, social media and print advertising. Look for cannabis publications and local hotspots where your target market frequents. If you run a business-to-business operation, develop relationships through mailers, cold email and even LinkedIn.

- Hiring employees. Make job postings on websites like Indeed, Craigslist, Monster, LinkedIn, CareerBuilder and ZipRecruiter. Create a page on your website that explains the type of employees you're looking for, and include a contact form. Ask your network for referrals.

- Find a payment processor. For a business in the cannabis industry, standard credit card processing companies will likely not work. You will need to look into merchants that accept high-risk businesses, such as CBD payment processors.

It can be challenging to start a business from the ground up. Stay patient and keep up with federal and state laws. In time, you could have a thriving cannabis business to be proud of.

You Want to Start a Cannabis Business: Advice for beginners

Interested in starting a business in the cannabis industry? I can't blame you business is booming and there's the potential to make huge profits as this sector continues to grow exponentially.

Over half of the United States already have legalized cannabis in some form that's 29 states plus the District of Columbia. Many states have only legalized cannabis for medical use, but that's gradually changing as well. Currently, one in five Americans lives in a state where they can use cannabis recreationally, without a doctor's note. In 2016, marijuana sales in North America grew by a massive 30 percent, and sales are projected to reach $20.2 billion by 2021. This is a huge deal, especially considering the industry is still in its infantile stages. There are still many gaps waiting to be filled by those who are forward-thinking and innovative enough to realize this is a once-in-a-generation opportunity. That said, the path to a successful cannabis business is not a smooth and easy one to navigate it's full of confusing laws and regulations, steep taxes, and many other unforeseeable roadblocks and hoops to jump through. That's why asked cannabis industry experts (who already have successful and profitable businesses!) for their top advice on starting a "cannabusiness." Their tips and information will give you a clearer road map and allow you to be more prepared for your exciting journey ahead.

Come up with a unique idea

When starting a business in any industry, having a unique idea that fills an unmet need is crucial to becoming a success. First, you'll need to decide which sector of the marijuana industry to go into. Generally, when someone thinks about types of cannabis businesses, dispensaries and grow operations usually come to mind.

Many see huge dispensaries in Colorado, for example, raking in big bucks. But this can actually be the riskiest business area to choose, with the tightest profit margins. As the legal use of marijuana continues to grow across the U.S., the price of weed will continue to go down, leaving those with grow-ops and dispensaries with fewer profits as time goes on. They're also the ones to be hit hardest with a sea of strict rules and regulations. On top of all of that, banks still refuse to work with businesses that grow or distribute marijuana because it is still illegal under federal law. This is sure to change eventually, but for now, you will still need to fundraise enough capital without any loan assistance. How much? Many states require proof of at least $1 million in available cash to obtain a dispensary license. You should also keep in mind that you won't be able to keep your profits safely stored in a bank account. All businesses that directly deal with cannabis are forced to keep their capital in cold hard cash, which is obviously highly inconvenient and dangerous though some have been getting around this issue using cryptocurrencies like bitcoin to keep their funds more secure.

But the cannabis industry is much more than just grow operations and dispensaries.

If you're a foodie, perhaps look into making a unique edibles line. There are even people opening up "bud and breakfasts" cannabis-friendly lodging

But truly, the least risky kind of cannabis business to start is one that doesn't directly touch the controversial plant at all. According to the Controlled Substances Act, the bulk of the regulations for businesses in the cannabis industry are only applicable to cannabis growers, processors, and sellers. This is why ancillary marijuana businesses are doing so well they aren't burdened with all the red tape and high taxes. From hydroponics and cultivation products to professional training and education, consultancies, media companies, the plethora of new technologies the list is endless, and so are the opportunities. If you're technical and a savvy inventor, you could design a product that helps marijuana user process or ingest their medicine think about all the fancy vape pens that have been coming out, or the rosin presses that easily extract solvent-free oil from bud or trim. Mike Bologna, CEO of Green Lion Partners, a Denver-based business strategy firm focused on early-stage development amongst firms in the cannabis industry, explains how essential a viable business idea is for aspiring cannabis entrepreneurs:

"When considering starting a business in the cannabis industry, entrepreneurs must first ensure their concept is legally viable and offers a unique solution for the space.

Too frequently, a concept is exciting but cannot be supported within the legal framework or is simply a recycled concept that is reliant upon 'first mover' advantage in their jurisdiction.

For long-term scalable success, a company must be able to withstand the dynamic regulations and business factors in this rapidly changing space."Marijuana Business Daily put out a useful chart showing the profitability of each type of cannabis business.

Understand your consumer base

Once you have a winning idea, it's vital to know who is going to be interested in your products or services and to deeply understand their particular wants and needs.

Bethany Gomez is director of research for Brightfield Group, a cannabis-focused market research firm providing accurate and comprehensive consumer, brand, and market insights in the industry. Here's what she has to say on the matter:

"When starting a cannabis business, two things are crucial: understanding the unique challenges of this industry and understanding your consumer base and the unmet need you are filling for them.

The cannabis industry is unlike any industry you have ever worked in, and the regulatory, supply chain, banking, taxation, advertising, and stigma aspects of the business eat your profits and draw your attention away from core aspects of your business. The legal cannabis space is becoming crowded and targeted consumer segmentation is increasingly important, so it's key to understand who your core consumers are and what they want from their products."

So get out there and do research on how you can ensure your future customers are happy and satisfied with what you offer them. Really get to know and understand them. Build a relationship with them. Do this, and you will develop a loyal consumer base. Krista Whitley, CEO of Altitude Products, a Las Vegas-based conglomerate of cannabis companies such as Social Media Unicorn, a canna-brand marketing and sales agency, and the Vegas Weekend Box, a monthly variety box of Las Vegas' top cannabis products, agrees that a good relationship with your consumers is essential:

"Success in the cannabis industry is uniquely tied to the connection and brand that leadership has with the local cannabis community.

It doesn't matter if you're starting your cannabis business in Washington, Colorado, or Maine; you should start by building authentic relationships with your local cannabis community."

Know the rules (and follow them!)

Even if you have a brilliant business plan, plenty of funding, and excited consumers that want what you're offering, if you don't play by the rules, you're going to get shut down, get hefty fines, and could even go to jail. Let's try to avoid that, yes? The laws, rules, and regulations for opening a cannabis business are incredibly confusing and complex. For example, even setting up a means of accepting payments can be trickyIt's recommended to hire an experienced attorney to aid you in navigating this process to make sure your business is legit. Each state has different laws.

"Both medical and adult-use businesses require, in most states, a license to operate, which is generally valid in just one state. Thus, your plan needs to comply with state law. The application process will give you a roadmap and likely where you can operate," explains Norman Olson, director of marketing and Business Affairs at Hightech Extracts, an engineering company developing systems for the manufacturing of extract-based products. "Funding and differentiating your service or brand will definitely help. Pick any consultant you engage only after thorough reference and background checks. Smoking a joint does not make you a cannabis expert!"

If you are irresponsible with your new cannabusiness, not only can this cause huge problems for you, but also for the cannabis industry as a whole. When businesses are performing reckless practices, it hurts the reputation of this new industry that still has many negative stigmas against it from the wider public.

Arnaud Dumas de Rauly, chief strategy officer for The Blinc Group, the first business incubator for brands specializing in vaporizer and cannabis consumption technologies, advises new cannabis-related businesses to understand the space and pay close attention to industry best practices:

"The cannabis industry is new and not yet fully regulated, making it very important for people entering the space to get in touch with their local institutions and industry groups and follow their guidance wisely.

The vaping industry was in a similar position a few years ago, and it's now facing huge regulatory challenges, some specifically caused by entrepreneurs that didn't take the time to do things right when first setting up their businesses, such as not acquiring licenses, using bad branding, labeling, and sales channels, and marketing to children. For the cannabis industry to grow properly, it'll need to avoid giving extra ammunition to regulatory agencies and opposition groups that seek to destroy it."

Raise enough capital

With any startup, investment capital is crucial to getting your business plan off the ground. Some investors don't want to put their money into cannabis businesses since it's still illegal under federal law. And, as stated earlier, forget about asking the bank to fund your marijuana business. Focus on finding some great private investors. While some are still wary, there are many investors out there excited about how fast the marijuana industry is exploding with growth, and they want in on the action. Dr. Andrew Kerklaan, president and founder of Dr. Kerklaan Therapeutics, a robust line of doctor-designed, lab-tested, patient-approved cannabis products that provide pain relief, sleep aid, PMS relief, and skin health, agrees:

"The days of bootstrapping a start-up in the cannabis industry are quickly coming to an end, if not already over.

My advice is to raise smart money with investors who can bring experience and expertise from other industries to the table.

Raise enough capital to quickly be able to compete."

Work hard and have fun!

It's a very exciting time to get involved in the cannabis industry. There are boundless opportunities to collaborate with a huge variety of businesses. Hopefully, now you have more of a solid idea of what it takes to start a business in the marijuana industry. Those willing to work hard and play by the rules have the potential to be extremely successful. Follow these guidelines and you will be well on your way to having a profitable business in the cannabis industry.

How to Successfully Launch a Legal Cannabis Business

Legal cannabis is one of the fastest-growing industries in the U.S.

The cannabis industry is newly legal, and as the industry shifts from the black market into the mainstream, it has experienced unprecedented growth. Building an industry from the ground up takes a lot of hands; the cannabis industry has attracted entrepreneurs of all stripes, from cultivators to distributors to tech experts, all of whom want a piece of the multibillion-dollar pie. While the industry has already experienced rapid growth, projections suggest it is still in its early stages. With seemingly nowhere to go but up, you might be considering launching a marijuana business of your own. The cannabis industry is a complicated space, due to both its youth and the legal circumstances surrounding it. This cannabis industry startup guide will provide a bird's-eye view of some things you should know about the marijuana business before launching a company of your own. Whether you're planning on opening a dispensary, obtaining a cultivation license or running an ancillary business, knowing the basics of the industry is essential to building a successful legal marijuana business.

The birth of an industry

Medical marijuana is legal in 33 states plus Washington, D.C., while adult-use cannabis (sometimes called "recreational marijuana") is legal in 10 states plus D.C. An additional 15 states have decriminalized cannabis, reducing possession under certain amounts to a civil charge rather than a criminal one. The rash of legalizations began with California's passage of medicinal cannabis measure Proposition 215 in 1996 and culminated in Colorado and Washington's legalization of recreational cannabis in 2012. Since then, more states have followed suit. In just 20 years, what was previously a black-market product has become the cash crop of a new industry. However, as the cannabis industry rises to prominence – multiple estimates place anticipated growth eclipsing the $20 billion mark by the early 2020s the federal government maintains cannabis as a Schedule 1 controlled substance. That means cannabis is considered an illegal substance with no accepted medical use and a high potential for abuse. Despite the federal prohibition, the cannabis industry grew and thrived largely on the back of the Department of Justice's 2013 missive known as the Cole Memorandum, which stated the feds would not interfere with cannabis operations that abide by their state's legal framework. The Cole Memorandum was rescinded by former U.S. Attorney General Jeff Sessions in 2018, but the industry remains protected by a hands-off culture among prosecutors, as well as a congressional measure known as the Rohrabacher-Blumenauer amendment that protects the medical cannabis industry. Rohrabacher-Blumenauer essentially states that no federal dollars will be appropriated for enforcement actions against state-compliant medical cannabis businesses. Unfortunately, even with these protections, the federal prohibition continues to create obstacles for legal cannabis businesses in other ways.

Even with this albatross around its neck, the legal cannabis industry is a burgeoning one. According to industry analysts New Frontier Data, the U.S. cannabis industry was worth $10.4 billion in 2018. That value is projected to grow rapidly through 2025 to $26.3 billion. Already, the cannabis industry has directly created nearly 300,000 jobs, not counting those indirectly created by support businesses like marketing companies or professional advisors.

A variety of business

With big numbers like $10.4 billion in value, you might be thinking the window of opportunity has mostly closed, but industry insiders told business.com that it's still early in the game. Stuart Titus, Ph.D., president and CEO of industrial hemp company Medical Marijuana Inc., said startups of all stripes still have ample opportunity to launch, grow and succeed in the cannabis space.

"The whole industry itself is at the very ground-floor level," Titus said in an interview at the Cannabis World Congress & Business Exposition. "We're certainly nowhere near maximizing what we could do. Look at alcohol prohibition. Suddenly, legalization spurred industries and businesses ... We think the same is true for this industry."

Cannabis businesses come in all shapes and sizes. Most people think of massive cultivation operations or dispensaries with jars full of shimmering emerald buds. Those are certainly key elements of the industry;

however, many cannabis entrepreneurs never even touch the plant itself. These include logistical support businesses, like distribution and transportation companies, or technology companies, such as dispensary software development or high-tech infrastructure for grow houses.

Science is also a huge driver of the cannabis industry, as it is in other agricultural endeavors. Labs are needed for testing the potency and genetics of cannabis flowers, extractors are required for harvesting oils, and ongoing research provides insights into the specifics of cannabis for medical treatment. Glass blowers, vape purveyors and edibles creators are also in high demand.

Regulatory landscape

The state of the industry remains very much in flux. Beyond the federal prohibition, or perhaps because of it, varying state frameworks have led to a fragmented industry that looks very different based on geography. Everything from licensing to reporting can be vastly different between states, making it difficult for a company to expand. Experience gained in Colorado, for example, does not necessarily translate to the New York market. "Since we're not a federally recognized industry, there are many things that are affected," said Sara Gullickson, CEO of DispensaryPermits.com, a consulting service for marijuana entrepreneurs. "In terms of regulations, every single state program varies. They're crafting programs specifically for their environment. So, things that are important in Arkansas might not be as important in Ohio, and so we're seeing that kind of flesh out." As knowledge of the industry improves, newer markets are including mandates that don't exist in older markets. For example, Gullickson said, Arizona's legal cannabis program includes no mention of testing, while newer markets mandate testing to ensure that cannabis is a safe, quality medical product for patients to use before it hits the market. The lack of federal policy has created a sort of experimental period, where states are borrowing what works from one another and trying to scrap what doesn't, Gullickson said. While the federal prohibition creates a lot of confusion and many problems, this trial-and-error period has been a good thing for the industry's evolution in her estimation.

"I'm a little bit more optimistic than most," Gullickson said. "I almost think if the feds stepped in and pushed something down everybody's throat, there'd be a lot of resistance. How could the feds come up with something that's uniform, implemented across the U.S., that works in every state? It's something that's necessary but also scary, because we do know what we're doing in different states and there are some really good programs. We don't want something to come into play that diminishes what good we're already doing."

Taxation

Since cannabis remains federally illegal, cannabis companies face different taxation challenges from other industries. Most notorious of these challenges is the Internal

Revenue Service's Section 280E, which does not allow cannabis companies to deduct ordinary business expenses from their tax bills. Section 280E was born of a 1981 court case in which a convicted drug dealer successfully wrote off his business expenses related to his illicit activities. Shortly after, Congress enacted Section 280E to avoid a repeat incident. Section 280E stipulates that any expenses related to the "trafficking of controlled substances" shall not be eligible for deductions or credits. Since cannabis remains a controlled substance under federal law, state-compliant legal cannabis businesses are subject to this tax rule. The result is that cannabis businesses pay a larger amount in taxes than they would if they sold a federally legal product. Cannabis companies must pay taxes based on their gross income, rather than their income minus cost of goods sold. The result is an average effective tax rate of 55% on cannabis businesses, compared with an average effective rate of 30% on similarly situated non-cannabis companies.

Beyond the federal tax code, cannabis companies must abide by various state tax plans. Some states charge excise taxes on top of their normal tax structure, such as Washington, where cannabis companies owe an excise tax of 37% on all sales. Your tax obligations as a cannabis business owner are significant and sometimes complex, so be sure to familiarize yourself with both federal and state tax policies.

Licensing and permitting

For businesses that touch the plant, licensing and permitting is essential. The process varies by state and can be rather arduous. In addition to outlining policies and procedures, applicants must provide an overview of who comprises their organization and to prove that what they say is true. According to Gullickson, balancing a level of detail in applications of limited length has become a skill set of its own in the consulting industry.

"About three or four years ago, when you were sending applications, everyone threw in the kitchen sink – thousands and thousands of pages to confuse people and hope they wouldn't read it," she said. "Now, the application process is often to describe in five pages what your operation looks like. You need someone to communicate to an uneducated audience what your policies and procedures look like. We had to sharpen our skill set to be as granular as possible in limited characters."

Ultimately, cultivators and dispensaries looking to score a license should be prepared to spend between $150,000 and $200,000 navigating the process, Gullickson said. For larger companies aiming for a sort of "super license," costs balloon from $500,000 to $750,000.

Banking and finance

Another problem caused by the federal prohibition centers on banking. Many banks are hesitant to do business with cannabis-related companies, while others refuse outright. Working with cannabis businesses is a risk for banks: On one hand, it opens the bank up to additional oversight and liability; on the other, there is a palpable fear that a federal crackdown could result in seized assets and a business catastrophe. The lack of conventional banking options has led cannabis entrepreneurs, especially those who touch the plant, to work primarily in cash. Not only is that dangerous – cannabis entrepreneurs are regularly targeted for robberies but tracking cash payments for tax and regulatory purposes is incredibly difficult.

"It's crippling right now," said Keegan Peterson, CEO of payroll and HR company Wurk. "You don't realize how important banking is until you don't have it just giving employees a paycheck is just brutal. In a cash environment, it's difficult to even prove you paid [your employees], or your vendors, or your tax liability." Moreover, cannabis businesses are often unable to open a traditional line of credit, limiting a common early-stage option for additional growth financing. That means bootstrapping or raising money from friends, families and angel investors is the most common way young companies gain a foothold. Luckily, the industry has developed some workarounds in the meantime. Angel investors willing to take the risk provide a lot of startup and growth capital, and several startup accelerators and incubators have burst onto the scene to help their cohorts get to the next level.

Venture capital firms tend to play it closer to the vest but are also intently watching the industry and making some preliminary investments. Still, the industry is holding its collective breath in hopes that the federal prohibition will soon be lifted, opening access to traditional banking and improving cannabis's already immense growth prospects. David Goldstein, CEO and co-founder of medical cannabis software company PotBotics, said it's important for a startup to allocate resources effectively, whether conventional banking becomes available soon or not. He also advised newcomers to bring in people with professional expertise elsewhere who can apply their knowledge to the cannabis industry. "What we see is that it's been tough to get institutional investment," he said. "Wealthy individuals that are passionate either because they went through chemo and cannabis helped or because they see the growth potential – those are the two types of investors we see. I think institutional money is coming but it's important for a startup to run lean but at same time bring in people who maybe worked in other industries so they can add their expertise to bring this out of [the] black market into white collar."

Frequently asked questions about starting a cannabis business

Looking for information not provided in the above cannabis industry startup guide? These FAQs might help you get started on the path to opening your own cannabis business, whether it's plant-touching or ancillary.

What is an ancillary cannabis business?

The term "ancillary cannabis business" refers to a company that provides needed services in the cannabis industry without actually touching the plant. These can be marketing agencies, professional advisors, payment processors, security companies and more. Ancillary businesses tend to provide B2B services to other cannabis companies. Ancillary businesses tend to avoid the onerous licensing and permitting requirements of plant-touching businesses. Many entrepreneurs entering the cannabis industry are pivoting their existing skill set or business and adapting it to the industry to provide necessary services.

How much does it cost to open a dispensary?

The cost of opening a cannabis dispensary depends on many factors, including your location, the size of your dispensary, and your state's application and licensing process. In some cases, opening a cannabis dispensary could be a multimillion-dollar process, while in others it could cost a few hundred thousand. The bottom line is that opening a cannabis dispensary isn't cheap. Moreover, it is a detailed and complicated process that requires meticulous planning. If you're considering opening a dispensary, it is important to line up the right partners, obtain funding and familiarize yourself with your state's application process. Every state will look for slightly different things, so it's important to optimize your plan based on what the state is looking for in an applicant.

How much does it cost to start a cannabis grow house?

Similar to opening a dispensary, launching a cannabis cultivation operation is no cheap endeavor. Estimates for the total initial investment for a 7,700-square-foot facility with 1,000 plants suggest it could cost more than $800,000, and certainly many cultivation operations become multimillion-dollar investments. Also similar to opening a dispensary is navigating the licensing process; it's important to understand what your state is looking for in an applicant and then building your team and business plan to suit those needs.

Where do you obtain a cannabis cultivation license?

To obtain a cannabis cultivation license, you will have to go through the regulatory body in your state. Typically, this is some kind of marijuana control board, but the exact process varies from state to state. Some states require your operation be vertically integrated, for example, meaning that you cultivate and sell your cannabis products from start to finish. Other states separate cultivation and dispensary licenses, meaning your company can only do one or the other.

What other permits does your marijuana business need?

Depending on where your business falls in the cannabis supply chain, you could require some other permits or licenses as well. In addition to cultivation and retail licenses for grows and dispensaries, there are processor licenses for value-added companies like extractors or edibles businesses, research licenses, and transportation licenses. Before launching your business, be sure to familiarize yourself with all the requirements of your state's law and to obtain all necessary licensing and permits before beginning operations.

How can I guarantee my cannabis business will be licensed?

There is no guarantee your cannabis business will be licensed but following your state's guidelines to the best of your ability will increase your chances. A strong team and good business plan are a must, backed up by realistic financials and a source of funding that makes your project credible. Some states prioritize social justice and diversity, giving a boost to teams led by minorities and veterans. Identifying the specific priorities of your state's regulators and tailoring your company and plan to suit them greatly increases your chance of getting a license; however, obtaining a license is never a guarantee.

How can entrepreneurs learn the cannabis laws?

Besides conducting your own research, it is critical to engage an experienced attorney when starting a cannabis business. Ideally, you will want to develop a relationship with an attorney who helps educate you on the applicable laws. Entering the cannabis industry without legal counsel is especially risky given the ever-changing laws from state to state and the uncertain future of federal policy.

How do you start a cannabis transport or logistics business?

To launch a transport or logistics business for the distribution of cannabis and cannabis products, you will likely require a transportation license. In some states, direct-to-consumer cannabis delivery is legal, while in other states it is not. Regardless, every legal cannabis company will need transportation for moving harvested product to processing facilities and dispensaries. Again, every state has its own specific rules and regulations regarding cannabis transport, so do your homework and follow all available guidelines.

Cannabis Laws

Cannabis has a lengthy and complicated history in the United States, to say the least. The use, sale, and possession of cannabis is illegal under federal law. However, individual states have enacted their own laws that often contradict the federal position. In fact, the states that outlaw even medical marijuana use are far outnumbered by those in which the opposite is true. For some people, it may feel like cannabis use has been effectively normalized. However, even states where marijuana is fully legal have different policies regarding accessibility, criminalization, and sale. Plus, because of the federal laws outlawing cannabis, banking for those businesses in this industry remains a sticky issue.

KEY TAKEAWAYS

- As of April 2021, 36 states and the District of Columbia have legalized marijuana use in some form.
- The Controlled Substances Act classified marijuana as a Schedule I drug, meaning it is considered to have "high abuse potential with no accepted medical use" under U.S. federal law.
- Any marijuana products with 0.3% or more delta-9-tetrahydrocannabinol (THC) is still technically illegal within the United States.

- When providing financial services to marijuana businesses, banks and institutions have to consider compliance costs, legal costs, logistical costs, educational costs, and reputational costs.

Marijuana Legalization in the U.S.

Prior to its more common association in the U.S. as a recreation substance, hemp crops were commonly grown during America's Colonial Era and the Early Republic, even by George Washington. However, the passage of the 1937 Marihuana Tax Act ultimately spelled the end of the hemp industry in the U.S. By 1970, the Controlled Substances Act had classified marijuana as a Schedule I drug, which means that it is considered to have "high abuse potential with no accepted medical use" under federal law. Although the Agriculture Improvement Act of 2018 removed certain cannabis products (including hemp) from the Controlled Substances Act, making them legal to produce and market, anything with 0.3% or more delta-9-tetrahydrocannabinol (THC) is still federally illegal.In spite of this, several state and local governments have passed their own laws to allow the use of marijuana products, though some restrictions may apply.

Marijuana Businesses and Banking

A cannabis dispensary is a location regulated by the local government where marijuana-based products may be purchased. Even if it is illegal to sell recreational marijuana in a particular state, licensed dispensaries still can. This is particularly applicable in states with legalized medical marijuana. Also, these locations shouldn't be confused with "head shops," as only paraphernalia can be purchased in these retail outlets. Getting licensed in any state to become a dispensary is often expensive, and ensuring you stay in legal compliance with local regulations is complicated because the rules change over time. They often require background checks for owners, employees, and investors. For anyone thinking of starting a dispensary, it is essential to perform a ton of research on existing and hypothetical laws, track down compliant rental properties, and potentially grow the actual product yourself. Another complicating factor to this risky business is that financing options are limited. Due to the current federal laws surrounding marijuana, it's difficult for most cannabis businesses to secure the proper financing and to find a bank that will take their business. Federally-insured credit unions and banks take significant risks if they choose to work with marijuana companies, even if the substance is legal under local law. Financial transactions involving proceeds generated from marijuana sales could result in prosecution under money laundering statutes, unlicensed money transmitter statutes, or the Bank Secrecy Act (BSA).Despite the risk, approximately 715 banks and credit unions are working with cannabis businesses. Numerica was one of the first financial institutions to offer its services to the marijuana industry, in 2014. Other credit unions, such as Salal,

Partner Colorado, and MAPS, followed soon after. Outside of credit unions, Timberland is another example of a bank that works with the cannabis industry.

When providing financial services to marijuana businesses, there are five key costs that banks and credit unions have to keep in mind:

- Compliance costs: Constantly changing regulatory and legislative policies make it difficult for even the most scrupulous of cannabis-related companies to operate totally on the level. As such, financial institutions have to invest a lot of time and money to ensure that their partners aren't engaged in anything potentially illegal, intentionally or not.
- Legal costs: Beyond financial liability for the actions of their partners, banks

and credit unions must consider hiring legal counsel for consulting, in-house compliance management, and handling the often protracted proceedings resulting from lawsuits.

- Educational costs: Given that this is a relatively new field, hiring outside help to ensure employees understand the intricacies of the marijuana industry can mean the difference between paying a little at the outset versus paying a lot down the road.
- Logistical costs: An almost entirely cash-based business model comes with a lot of risks and complications, ranging from needing to hire additional security to be forced to work with expensive vendors.

- Reputational costs: Even if marijuana is legal in a state, the financial institutions that chose to work with cannabis-related businesses are likely to still face criticism from their partners or members who disapprove of the substance's use as a recreational substance or who disapprove out of federal legal concerns.

Introduced in 2019, the Secure and Fair Enforcement (SAFE) Banking Act could be the silver bullet solution to the difficulties that discourage most banks and credit unions from doing business with the cannabis industry, according to its supporters. This bill is designed to prevent "a federal banking regulator from penalizing a depository institution for providing banking services to a legitimate marijuana-related business." The bill received the two-thirds majority vote required to pass the House in September 2019 The bill then moved on to Senate for consideration, where progress has essentially stalled. In addition to facing an unfriendly Republican majority, Senate Banking Committee Chair, Mike Crap, has proved more interested in introducing his own legislation to address marijuana banking concerns specifically something that would provide more protection for hemp and CBD businesses as well as ban high-THC vapes and certain edibles.

States voting on cannabis legalization in 2020

Five states are confirmed to vote on some form of cannabis legalization during the

November 2020 election, with a sixth potentially joining depending on the result of a pending court decision.

- Arizona: In Arizona, voters will determine whether the state legalizes an adult-use cannabis program. Petitioners in Arizona collected more than 420,000 signatures and defeated a lawsuit to secure the ballot referendum. The state's adult-use cannabis market is expected to generate $750 million in value annually, according to Cannabis News Box.
- Mississippi: Voters in Mississippi will have multiple medical-marijuana-legalization referendums on the ballot in November. One, called Initiative 65, was developed through a grassroots campaign that gathered more than

105,000 signatures. A competing measure proposed by state legislators, known as Alternative 65A, will also be up for a vote. If approved, both measures would legalize medical marijuana, but regulatory details would vary.

- Montana: After petitioners gathered more than 130,000 signatures, Montana voters will have the chance to approve an adult-use cannabis program in a state that recently oversaw reform to its existing medical-marijuana program. In 2018, Montana's medical-marijuana program generated $45 million in sales; expanding the industry into the adult-use market would likely increase that value substantially.

- New Jersey: After several failed attempts to legalize adult-use cannabis through the state legislature, New Jersey is leaving it up to the voters this November. If the measure is approved, the state would have one of the lowest sales-tax rates placed on cannabis in the country. New Jersey's cannabis industry could be worth $1.5 billion annually if the measure passes, according to projections from Marijuana Business Daily.
- South Dakota: South Dakota voters will have the opportunity to vote for the legalization of both medical marijuana and adult-use cannabis. No other state has legalized both medical-cannabis and adult-use-cannabis programs at the same time.

Nebraska could potentially join these five states with a cannabis-legalization measure on the ballot. Petitioners looking to get a medical-marijuana-legalization referendum on the ballot collected 182,000 signatures — 60,000 more than required by Nebraska state law. However, Nebraska's push for a medical-cannabis vote has faced a challenge in court by Lancaster County Sheriff Terry Wagner. A final ruling on whether the referendum will be on the ballot is expected this fall.

High-Paying Jobs in the Marijuana Industry

When most people think of marijuana, they're likely to think of grow ops set up in secret backrooms of shady dealers. But things are changing, especially now that the stigma attached to using the plant begins to fade. The cannabis plant has been used for both medicinal and recreational purposes for as long as we can remember. But governments have only recently recognized and admitted that the physical and economic benefits outweigh the dangers of the drug. In fact, with more areas of the world legalizing usage, the marijuana industry is growing and rapidly innovating.

KEY TAKEAWAYS

- Medical marijuana is legal in some form in 35 states and the District of Columbia.
- The cannabis industry is expected to grow by as much as 14% by 2025,

according to a cannabis research group.

- Top roles in the field include consultant, dispensary executive, extraction technician, grow master, and edibles chef

Cannabis Consultant

Consulting is generally a high-paying career path, and the cannabis industry is no exception. Cannabis consultants can earn six figures by combining their expertise in state and local cannabis regulations with their backgrounds as lawyers, accountants, or people with experience in another area of the marijuana industry. They can help businesses find acceptable locations, obtain the licenses they need, and advise them on other legal matters so they don't get fined or shut down. They may also help business owners with bookkeeping and tax requirements, which can be especially tricky, as cannabis is generally a cash-only business due to its illegality at the federal level.

Dispensary COO and CFO

Work for a state-licensed medical marijuana dispensary as a chief operating officer (COO) or chief financial officer (CFO) and you could earn $125,000 a year, plus medical and retirement benefits. Job responsibilities may include:

- Managing cultivation facility operations
- Managing the company's accounting department
- Supervising financial reporting

Important terms in cannabis market

Access Point

An access point is a location where medical marijuana patients are authorized to buy or pick up cannabis. The term access point is often used somewhat interchangeably with the term dispensary. In either case, the location refers to a state-authorized facility that must abide by strict processes and guidelines.

Agitation

Agitation refers to a specific procedure in the process of harvesting marijuana plants and products. In agitation, producers utilize physical contact with marijuana plants in order to break off trichomes for collection and processing. Trichomes contain most of the marijuana plant's cannabinoids and other active compounds

Backcross

Successful marijuana production requires extensive knowledge of botany and biology, and backcrossing is an industry term borrowed from these fields. Producers backcross a marijuana plant when they facilitate plant breeding in such a way as to transfer one or more desired traits from a parent to an offspring. Specifically, this process typically entails breeding a plant with one of its parents in order to strengthen particular genes in rare strains.

BHO

BHO refers to butane hash oil, a potent cannabis concentrate made from marijuana plants using butane as a solvent. It contains extremely high amounts of THC, can be manufactured in a variety of ways, and can have different consistencies. It is also known as honey oil or earwax.

Bud

A marijuana plant bud is a flower found on mature plants. Buds contain high levels of cannabinoids, making them a popular choice for harvesting.

Cannabidiol

Cannabidiol, commonly abbreviated as CBD, is one of the dozens of molecules found in the cannabis plant which are referred to as cannabinoids. CBD has become popular in recent years due to a belief that it provides medical benefits for patients suffering from various afflictions including seizures, pain, arthritis, and more. CBD is unlike THC in that it does not contain psychoactive properties. This means that individuals can use CBD for its medical benefits without feeling high. CBD is most commonly delivered to users via oils, topical products, and tinctures.

Cannabinoids

This term refers to a large group of chemical compounds found in the cannabis plant. These compounds engage with receptors in the cells of the brain which are related to neurotransmission. The two best-known cannabinoids are tetrahydrocannabinol (THC) and CBD. THC is well-known for producing psychoactive effects in users of cannabis products—the compound responsible for the high associated with cannabis use. CBD is better known for its health effects and does not include a psychoactive component. Besides these two cannabinoids, there are dozens of other compounds in the various parts of a cannabis plant as well.

Concentrate

Concentrates are highly potent extracts from the cannabis plant that contain cannabinoids like THC. All the plant material is removed in the production process.

Common concentrates include hash, kief, and hash oils. They are used in both medical and recreational settings.

Cross

Multiple cannabis plants can be interbred to generate a new strain of product in a process known as crossbreeding or crossing for short. New strains of marijuana are produced in order to control for factors including appearance, potency, and more.

Crystals

The term crystals refers to trichomes a white, crystal-like part of the cannabis plant that contains high concentrations of THC. Crystals are used to produce various concentrates.

Dabbing

While smoking and ingesting cannabis-based products remain two of the most favored methods of consuming marijuana, a relatively new method called dabbing has become popular. To dab, a user places a small amount of a cannabis concentrate on a hot oil rig pipe. The concentrate is vaporized and the user then inhales the vapor.

Decarboxylation

Decarboxylation is a process used to transform certain inactive cannabinoids into active compounds like THC and CBD. The process involves the slow heating of marijuana at a low temperature and is commonly utilized to make edibles.

Dispensary

Stores that sell marijuana products are known as dispensaries. Some dispensaries may carry more than just marijuana itself, including items like paraphernalia or clothing as well. Because legal cannabis sales are governed differently depending upon the U.S. state or Canadian province, the specific requirements and the setup of a dispensary depend heavily on where it is located.

Edibles

Products containing cannabis-based chemicals are designed to be orally ingested are known as edibles. Some of the most popular edible products include baked goods, candy, and soda.

Feminization

The process of feminization results in cannabis seeds that produce only female plants. In the cannabis industry, female plants are often seen as more desirable than their male counterparts, because only female plants produce flowers. Producing only plants of one type also protects against undesired fertilization.

Germination

Germination is the part of the life cycle of a cannabis plant when the seed begins to sprout and develop into a seedling.

Hash

Also known as hashish, this is a highly potent concentrate of marijuana trichomes achieved by one of several extraction techniques.

Hemp

Hemp is a variety of the Cannabis Sativa plant. It contains very small traces of THC and high amounts of CBD. Hemp fibers are used in various industries including the textile, paper, and automobile industries. CBD is extracted from the plant for various uses. Growing hemp was illegal on a federal level in the U.S. up until December 2018. Then the 2018 Farm Bill lifted the ban so long as it contains a maximum of 0.3% THC.5

Hydroponics

A hydroponic system makes it possible to grow cannabis without the use of soil and increases the plant's growth rate. Specifically, hydroponic mechanisms circulate both water and essential nutrients to a cannabis plant's roots in order to facilitate growth.

Indica

There are three different species of cannabis plants—Indica, Sativa, and ruderalis. Indica cannabis plants tend to have dense clusters of buds and the strain is thought to have a sedative effect.

Kief

When trichomes are removed from a marijuana plant, kief is the result. It is a type of cannabis concentrate also known as dry sieve hash. Kief typically contains high concentrations of THC.

Live Resin

When a cannabis concentrate is made using freshly picked plants that are immediately harvested and frozen, the product is known as live resin.

QWISO

QWISO, or quick-wash isopropyl, is a method to make hash oil that involves the use of isopropyl alcohol to collect trichomes from a cannabis plant.

Resin

Resin is a term that is often used interchangeably with trichomes, though it also holds other meanings in the cannabis industry as well. After a piece of marijuana paraphernalia is used, the residue left inside is often referred to as resin as well.

Ruderalis

Along with Indica and Sativa, ruderalis is one of the three species of cannabis plants. Ruderalis plants are somewhat larger than Indica ones, and it also flowers on its own without stimulation from a light cycle. Ruderalis plants tend to have higher concentrations of CBD relative to Indica and Sativa.

Sativa

Sativa plants are the tallest of all the cannabis species, and the strain is often considered to enhance creativity and energy.

Shatter

Shatter is one of the consistencies found in butane hash oil. This product can be used for dabbing or can be smoked in combination with a flower.

Seed-to-Sale

Seed-to-sale is a term used to refer to the close watch cannabis companies have to keep on each step of the manufacturing process in order to comply with government regulations.

Topical

Topical products are among the newest forms of cannabis products. These include lotions and creams applied topically which aim to address issues like pain and skin problems. Even though some topicals contain THC, the method of absorption means they do not cause the high of other cannabis products.

Trichomes

Also known as crystals, trichomes are resin-producing glands on a marijuana plant.

They have the appearance of small hairs. Trichomes are responsible for producing the large majority of a cannabis plant's cannabinoids.

What types of financing are available for cannabis businesses?

Traditional loans are rare in the cannabis industry, because the FDIC will not back any bank that lends money to a business that breaks federal law, which all state-compliant legal cannabis companies currently do. While conventional loans can be nearly impossible to come by for cannabis businesses, funding sources are available. In addition to angel investors and venture capitalists, cannabis-specific funding companies have launched to fill the gap left by banks too hesitant to provide loans to young cannabis companies. Many ancillary cannabis companies are also bootstrapped, started from the owners' own savings or personal financing options.